# TOP TIPS:
# EXPLAINING THE CROSS

Helen Franklin, Steve Hutchinson, Robert Willoughby

Copyright © Scripture Union 2008
First published 2008
ISBN 978 184427 330 0

Scripture Union England and Wales
207-209 Queensway, Bletchley, Milton Keynes, MK2 2EB, England
Email: info@scriptureunion.org.uk
Website: www.scriptureunion.org.uk

Scripture Union Australia, Locked Bag 2, Central Coast Business Centre, NSW 2252
Website: www.scriptureunion.org.au

Scripture Union USA
PO Box 987, Valley Forge, PA 19482
Website: www.scriptureunion.org

British Library Cataloguing-in-Publication Data: a catalogue record of this book is available from the British Library.

Printed and bound in Singapore by Tien Wah Press Ltd

Logo, cover design, internal design: www.splash-design.co.uk

Internal illustrations: Colin Smithson

Typesetting: Richard Jefferson, Author and Publisher Services

Advisers: Colin Draper, John Grayston and John Marshall

Scripture Union is an international Christian charity working with churches in more than 130 countries, providing resources to bring the good news about Jesus Christ to children, young people and families and to encourage them to develop spiritually through the Bible and prayer.

As well as our network of volunteers, staff and associates who run holidays, church-based events and school Christian groups, we produce a wide range of publications and support those who use our resources through training programmes.

Children Matter! facilitates co-operation between all Christians who work with children. For more details see www.childrenmatter.net

# CONTENTS

Introduction                                                    4

Part One     What the Bible says about the cross               5

Part Two     Helping children make sense of the cross         13

Part Three   Explaining the cross in practice                 19

Ten Top Tips                                                   31

Resources                                                      32

# INTRODUCTION

It is mainly children with no church background who come to your midweek club. 'I don't get it!' says a 10-year-old boy. 'Why did Jesus die? He's supposed to be the hero!'…

The subject of the cross and Jesus' death can occur regularly in conversations that children's workers have with children. You want to explain the cross as clearly and relevantly as possible. You want them to understand and respond as appropriate.

This book explores what the Bible has to say about the cross; identifying four key ways to understand it biblically and then how these might make sense to children. It is followed by practical advice on communicating the amazing message of the cross in the most effective way. The immediate application is to those working with children, but much of it is relevant to those working with young people (and adults too!). This book is inevitably brief. Books about the Atonement can fill a book twenty times the size of this one. To find out more, turn to page 32.

Right at the start, two central truths about God need to be made clear. They are foundational to everything we might ever say to a child about the cross:

* **God loves the world**. John 3:16 says it best – 'For God so loved the world that he gave his one and only Son, that whoever believes in him shall not perish but have eternal life.' Indeed God IS love (1 John 4:7–21).

* **We don't deserve God's love**. Romans 3:23 says this best – 'For all have sinned and fall short of the glory of God.' Sin is not just about doing bad things but is about our very nature – what we are all like deep down. This may be unpopular language today but the Bible is clear: human beings, even children, are sinners. To repair our broken relationship with a loving God, we need a Saviour.

# PART I – WHAT THE BIBLE SAYS ABOUT THE CROSS

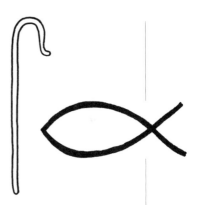

Christians have always used symbols to express their faith. For example, a boat, (from Jesus' first encounters with his disciples), is sometimes used to symbolise the church, or a dove sometimes represents the Holy Spirit, or the Good Shepherd or a fish. But none of these symbols has the central position which the cross holds for Christians, and an understanding of this vital aspect of Christian belief is essential, even for children.

When Paul wrote to the church at Corinth he stressed that, although some considered the cross foolishness and others found it a stumbling-block to faith, he had resolved to focus solely upon the cross as the single thing about Christianity which was absolutely key to their lives (1 Corinthians 1:18–2:5; Galatians 6:14). The understanding of the cross to Christians in bringing them to God is technically referred to as the Atonement.

Some people argue that Jesus' life or his teaching or the empty tomb are equally important, and we would have no desire to diminish their importance. The cross, however, is central. In Mark's story of the life of Jesus, it is clear from the beginning that Jesus is on a collision course which will end in his death (Mark 3:6). By the middle of the Gospel Jesus has pointed out that this was indeed his purpose in life (Mark 8:31; 9:31; 10:33,34). There was no other way.

Mark's story of Jesus' passion, including his arrest, trials before Jews and Romans, humiliation and crucifixion, is the climax of the gospel and fills two long chapters (Mark 14,15). Jesus prepares his disciples for his death at the Last Supper (Mark 14:22–25) by explaining, in the simple form of bread and wine, what his forthcoming death will mean for them. From this occasion Christians derive the central act of their worshipping lives – Holy Communion.

One of the things associated with Jesus' shedding his blood on the cross is the establishing of a new covenant, a new agreement with humanity, something which the prophet Jeremiah, in particular, predicted (Jeremiah 31:31–34). In the ancient world covenants were usually sealed by shedding blood to underline the very serious life-and-death nature of such a binding agreement (see, for example, Exodus 24). Even today we take covenants, such as treaties between nations and marriage between a man and woman, very seriously. They bind the participants to the promises made. God's seriousness of purpose in establishing this new covenant is demonstrated by the fact that it comes at the cost of the death of Jesus and the shedding of his own blood.

By the time of the apostle Paul, Christians were ready to look back at what had happened and tease out the meaning of the cross in a variety of different ways or models. Nothing could be more important for children than to explain to them the cross using ways that are appropriate, both for them to understand Jesus' life and death, and for them to experience true forgiveness and freedom. Classically, the four main ways have been described as penal substitution, reconciliation, Christ the Victor and redemption.

## Jesus the Sacrifice

This model comes first, not because it is the only one, but because it supports and lays the foundation for all of the others. It deals with the most basic of human problems – that of sin and the human need for forgiveness from God.

When he wrote to the Romans, Paul was faced with a divided church made up of Jewish and Gentile Christians. He wrote about how God, who is completely just, is angry at sin (Romans 1:18; 3:20). His first task was to show that everyone, Jews as well as Gentiles, falls short of God's standards and is a sinner (Romans 3:23). Since he is a just God, such sin must be punished. In ancient societies, including the Old Testament (eg Leviticus 16), a substitute could stand between God and the human sinner. This substitute usually took the form of an animal sacrifice. Paul tells us that Jesus became that sacrifice and that, at the cross, God himself was able to punish wrongdoing, whilst maintaining his own righteousness and acquitting guilty humanity (Romans 3:21–26; 8:3). Instead of condemning humanity, God now declares that they are righteous.

'This righteousness from God comes through faith in Jesus Christ to all who believe. There is no difference, for all have sinned and fall short of the glory of God, and are justified freely by his grace through the redemption that came by Christ Jesus. God presented him as a sacrifice of atonement, through faith in his blood.' (Romans 3:22–25.)

Later in Romans, Paul wrote, 'When we were still powerless, Christ died for the ungodly' (Romans 5:6). Hebrews 9:1 – 10:18 develops this model of Jesus as both the High Priest who offered the sacrifice, and the Sacrifice itself.

This model is sometimes related to the idea of penal substitution and is particularly helpful because it is reasonably easy to see how God deals with human sin with which he is angry. It offers the possibility of forgiveness, peace and friendship (Romans 5:1,10–11). The cross removes the major barrier between God and human beings. Romans goes on to describe the ensuing relationship with God as that of children adopted by their heavenly Father (Romans 8:15–17) who seek to live up to their new-found dignity and identity. The only way to acquire this status before God is by faith in Christ, which we often refer to as justification by faith.

Many Christians regard this as *the* foundational understanding of the cross as it highlights so many facets of what Jesus was achieving on the cross. This model has sometimes been caricatured as God taking it out on Jesus. Some have even labeled it 'cosmic child-abuse'. But this is to forget that the Trinity is not divided in any way. God is, at one and the same time, Judge and willing Victim who pays the penalty. No one, not even the Father, took Jesus' life from him (John 10:18).

## Jesus the Reconciler

When Paul wrote his second letter to the Christians in Corinth his relationship with them was badly strained. They had always been a difficult church, but things had got worse. What he wrote here is key to understanding the cross.

'Therefore, if anyone is in Christ, he is a new creation; the old has gone, the new has come! All this is from God, who reconciled us to himself through Christ and gave us the ministry of reconciliation: that God was reconciling the world to himself in Christ, not counting men's sins against them. And he has committed to us the message of reconciliation. We are therefore Christ's ambassadors, as though God were making his appeal through us. We implore you on Christ's behalf: Be reconciled to God. God made him who had no sin to be sin for us, so that in him we might become the righteousness of God. (2 Corinthians 5:17–21.)

**In reality...**
Playground feuds, classroom rivalries, bickering, being ignored by peers – and the satisfaction when broken relationships are mended – are all experiences deeply felt by children and young people. Ask them, to find out!

As was the case between Paul and the church in Corinth, the relationship between God and humanity has broken down badly because of sin. Paul meant that when Jesus was crucified, a loving God was bringing people back to himself as friends (2 Corinthians 5:19, Romans 5:10). This is often referred to as reconciliation. The implications of this are obvious because mending and renewing broken relationships, friendships and forgiveness are common experiences for all people of all ages.

## Jesus the Victor

When Paul wrote to the Christians at Colossae he was demonstrating that Christ was supreme over all sources of religious fear, tyranny, wisdom or salvation (however that might have been understood). In majestic terms he laid out exactly who Jesus is in his relationship to Almighty God. In Colossians 1:15–20 he wrote that Jesus not only existed from before the beginning of time, but even participated in the act of creation itself. So everything that exists owes its continuing being to him. Paul recognised, however, that all is not well between God and his creation. It was Jesus who reconciled everything to God on the cross and made peace between them. Paul explained this to the Colossians as follows:

> 'God made you alive with Christ. He forgave us all our sins, having cancelled the written code, with its regulations, that was against us and that stood opposed to us; he took it away, nailing it to the cross. And having disarmed the powers and authorities, he made a public spectacle of them, triumphing over them by the cross … Since you died with Christ to the basic principles of this world, why, as though you still belonged to it, do you submit to its rules…?' (Col 2:13–23)

Any supposed list of sins and shortcomings was cancelled (Colossians 2:14) and, as it were, nailed to the cross. Evil authorities, powers and so-called rulers were demolished. Jesus had triumphed on the cross. Nobody could point at these Christians to accuse them of spiritual failure for they were now on the winning side. Jesus had triumphed on their behalf. For that reason they didn't need to fear anyone or anything and could live in freedom from accusation of any sort. This is not to deny that they were still in a spiritual battle (Ephesians 6:10–20) but the outcome of that battle was already assured. They were winners.

## Jesus the Rescuer (Redeemer)

This model is based upon the story of the exodus when God's people were set free from slavery in Egypt. In Romans 3:24 Paul wrote that Jesus has freed us by taking away our sins. In other words, people are slaves to sin in the same way that the Israelites were slaves in Egypt. In both cases, something good was brought out of evil. Usually there is the idea that a price has to be paid in order to purchase freedom. Although this isn't clear in the story of the exodus, there is the evidence of the lamb's blood on the doorposts – evidence that a deal had been struck.

This is sometimes referred to as redemption, with Jesus as the Redeemer. The idea is that a price is paid, a ransom, to secure someone's freedom or release from bondage or even a particular debt. Jesus bought our forgiveness by giving up his life. As Mark 10:44,45 says:

'…whoever wants to be first must be slave of all. For even the Son of Man did not come to be saved, but to serve, and to give his life as a ransom for many.'

Like most models, it is possible to push this picture too far. For example, it is impossible to say with certainty to whom the debt is owed or paid.

People often use the word 'salvation' to describe the overall work of Jesus, which is especially close to this idea of redemption. Even if we have little direct

**In reality…**
The idea of being given money-off vouchers to exchange for a pizza or reduced price cinema ticket will be familiar to children.

experience of these things, most people can grasp the idea that we have been rescued, set free, saved or released from 'prison'.

**Don't forget the resurrection!**
All models for understanding the cross must include the resurrection. This is the vital conclusion to any presentation of the death of Christ. He was not just a tragic martyr or hero. Adults and, perhaps especially, children need to know a sense of the triumph which is achieved by God in the cross of Christ. The resurrection is that triumph. As Paul says, 'And if Christ has not been raised, your faith is futile; you are still in your sins.' (1 Corinthians 15:17).

**Understanding sin**
Sin is always about displeasing God and breaking his law. The four models of the cross address sin in a slightly different way.
*   Jesus the Sacrifice: Sin is pollution and needs a sacrifice to cleanse the sinner.
*   Jesus the Reconciler: Sin is a broken relationship with God on the part of the sinner which Jesus heals.
*   Jesus the Victor: Sin is seen as an oppressive force which binds up the sinner whom Jesus liberates.
*   Jesus the Rescuer: Sin is seen as slavery from which Jesus delivers the sinner.

**Think about...**
Which understanding of sin strikes you as most helpful when speaking with children? (Probably more than one!)

# PART TWO – HELPING CHILDREN MAKE SENSE OF THE CROSS

## 2

## Jesus the Sacrifice dying instead of me

To children in the 21st century, sacrifice in a religious context is a hard concept. But the idea of someone taking the blame for someone else is easily understood. 'Who did it?' 'Not me, Sir!' Someone is at fault and should take the blame. This can be taken further to when someone is blamed and takes the punishment for another person's wrongdoing, even though they have done nothing wrong. Ultimately this is what Jesus did, acting as a substitute and facing the anger of God the Father as he hung on the cross. In desolation he shouted out, 'My God, my God, why have you deserted me?' (Mark 15:34).

But how can a child grasp such a devastating act? It is like a child who loves their parent and knows they are loved, but experiences that parent turning away from them, refusing to help in a time of need. It is a mystery but the grief that God the Father experienced cannot be underestimated.

Children can understand that something pure can become contaminated. God, who is pure, could not be associated with Jesus who, at the point of hanging on the cross and taking our wrongdoing upon himself, had become utterly impure (see 1 Peter 2:24). Again this is a mystery!

Children are acutely aware of fairness and justice. In one sense, it was not fair that Jesus died. He had done no wrong. But someone had to be punished for human wrongdoing. That's how God had said it was to be. The story of the repentant thief dying on the cross next to Jesus is a clear statement of the injustice of Jesus' death and Jesus dying for someone else (Luke 23:32–43). The thief on the cross recognised that he and the other thief deserved to die, but not Jesus.

We need to be cautious in how we use the term 'substitute'. The image in the Bible is very different from the one in sport where a substitute often comes on when someone is injured. However, a substitute may be brought on to swing the outcome of the game, which in one sense is what Jesus did. See page 18 for an example of a prayer of response to this explanation of the cross.

## Jesus the Reconciler: Jesus the Friend

Probably the easiest explanation of the cross for a child to understand is that of reconciliation – all about relationships and God making us his friends (Romans 5:10). Most children experience the love of family or friends, learning to say sorry when something they have done damages a relationship. To be accepted by someone who loves you is a basic human need. Sadly, unconditional parental love is not the experience of all children. Core to the Christian message is that God loves and values everyone, including all children and young people, and he does that unconditionally. But our wrong attitudes, behaviour and deliberate ignoring of Jesus have damaged that relationship. Of course, many children may not be aware of a relationship with God because the members of their family ignore him.

If something has gone wrong in a relationship, someone may be needed to bring the two sides together. Children will be aware of a teacher bringing two children together who have had a disagreement. Children caught up in a family divorce may be very aware of the role of those seeking to reconcile. Older children may be involved in peer mentoring, where they are trained to sort out playground disputes requiring a go-between or a reconciler. In situations of war, there are peacemakers.

So it is with the broken relationship between us and God. Although he has done nothing to cause the rift, he has provided the one who comes to bring the two sides together, the Reconciler. Younger children find it hard to grasp how grieved God is by the wrong we have done. But they can, in a simple way, see the need to say sorry if we wish to be friends with God, when we have done wrong. Jesus has come to make us friends with God which is what he did on the cross. This model emphasises God's love for us. A prayer of response to this explanation of the cross is on page 18.

## Jesus the Victor:

Many well known stories for adults and children, for example, *Lord of the Rings*, are based on the battle between good and evil. The whole of Jesus' life can be seen as such a battle. On the cross Jesus proved he had power over all evil.

For many children the world is a scary place. Ask any child who is bullied or any young person with a concern about climate change or the effects of war. Children need to know that God is not a distant, powerless being but is someone personally involved in them and in their world, able to stand up for them. This is why the resurrection is so important. Jesus' death was not the end; he overcame death. What is more, having gone back to heaven, he is alive today in our world, by the Spirit. If children welcome him, he is alive in them too. His power included nailing the punishment for our wrongdoing on the cross and taking it away (Colossians 2:14,15). This way of explaining the cross emphasises God's great power. In effect, children are invited to swap sides, joining God's team or army – a guarantee of victory.

Jesus' shout on the cross, 'It is finished' (John 19:30), didn't mean that he was finished, but that the battle against the forces of evil had been decided. To prove it, God raised him back to life as the victor over sin, death and evil. A prayer of response to this explanation of the cross is on page 18.

## Jesus the Rescuer

The idea of someone being kidnapped with money demanded for their release is familiar. The idea of a rescuer may be even more accessible for children, whether it's a firefighter saving a child from a blazing inferno, or the crew of a lifeboat, especially if they put their own life at risk. Jesus comes to us in times of need. Ultimately, he came to rescue people from the dangerous consequences of sin. The story of Zacchaeus demonstrates this clearly (Luke 19:1–10). Zacchaeus was caught up in a lifestyle of dishonesty and was a lonely outcast. Jesus came to rescue him – to seek and to save one of the lost!

This is not straightforward for it relies on making a jump from someone being physically held as a captive to the more abstract idea of being held captive by sin, with Jesus dying to pay the ransom price so that we can be set free. But since the idea of rescue and saving is core to our understanding of the cross, this is a very powerful Biblical model for children. It does not especially emphasise the role of personal repentance. Children can call upon Jesus to protect and rescue them even though they may not fully understand the implications of their sin. A prayer of response to this explanation of the cross is on the next page.

Children will respond to each of these four models (and others, such as a demonstration of God's great love) in different ways and at different times. Long term it is never enough to only respond to one. All people need to know Jesus as their victor, saviour, rescuer, friend, reconciler, redeemer, king, substitute, and so on.

**Think about...**
Which, if any, of these models most influenced you when you first became aware of your relationship with God? How might your experience affect how you explain the cross to children? Many would say they were not aware of their need for repentance until much later in their lives.

## MODELS OF THE CROSS

These prayers of response show how each way of seeing the cross might prompt a different response. It may not be appropriate to use these exact words.

(References to the crucifixion are not included in the Bible verses column.)

| Model of the cross | Key Bible verses` | Key words | Suggested prayer of response with this model |
|---|---|---|---|
| Jesus the Sacrifice (penal substitution) | Rom 1:18; 3: 20–26; 5:6; 8:3; Heb 9:1–10:18; 1 Pet 2:24 | sacrifice, victim, high priest, substitute, punishment, justice, blame | Lord God, thank you that Jesus took the blame for what I've done wrong when he died on the cross. I am sorry for the wrong things I have done, said and thought. Please forgive me and make me the type of person you want me to be, living in a way that pleases you. |
| Jesus the Reconciler | Rom 5:10; 2 Cor 5:19 | friend, love, broken relationship, bring together, forgiveness | Father God, I know I have done, said and thought things that have spoilt my relationship with you. I am sorry. Thank you that Jesus died on the cross to make it possible for me to become your friend. Please forgive me and help me live as your friend from now on. |
| Jesus the Victor | Col 2:13–23; Eph 6:10–20, John 19:30 | evil powers, fear, bullying, powerless, champion, goodness, victory | Victorious Jesus, your power is so great that I come to you for protection. Thank you that when you died on the cross and came alive again, you showed that you are stronger than all evil. Please take away the wrong in me and may your power help me live to please you. |
| Jesus the Rescuer (Redeemer, Ransom) | Exod 12; Rom 3:24; Mark 10:45; Luke 19:1–10 | ransom, redeemer, saviour, freedom, prisoner | Jesus Christ, you came to rescue people who needed you. That's why you died on the cross to pay for the wrong things that stop me from being the person you made me to be. Thank you for rescuing me and now help me to live in a way that pleases you. |

# PART THREE – EXPLAINING THE CROSS IN PRACTICE

## 3

## Age considerations

Death is a difficult concept to explain to any child. But we shouldn't be afraid to talk about how Jesus died on a cross. Children need to know that it happened, even though it may be several years before they can fully understand.

With very young children, you could explain the Easter story as a 'Sad/Happy' one – Mary Magdalene's deep sadness turning to joy. Older children understand more about death and ways of dying. They learn about the Romans and have more ability to understand the context of Jesus' crucifixion. They may still struggle with abstract ideas and making a link between Jesus' death and its significance to all people. They may be moved emotionally, particularly if they have come to count themselves as friends of Jesus. We need to listen carefully to their concerns, as they work it out for themselves.

As children approach their teens, they may have a growing awareness of their own sin. It can be useful to speak of sin in terms of the factors that cause relationships to be broken. Being part of and accepted by a peer group can be so important. Exclusion from such a group is painful. Young people may be concerned that they can never be good enough to be friends with Jesus because of the wrong they have done (which is different from having a poor self-image). If they mess up badly they may feel they can't be forgiven. They need reassurance, both of our love and acceptance, and of God's.

## Telling the story

It is obviously important that children and young people hear the story of the cross and resurrection in an appropriate way for their age and life experience. Younger children should be spared the horror. It is

**Think about...**
Use a picture of three crosses. When one criminal insults Jesus and the other tells him off, fix cards labelled 'Done Wrong' to the outer crosses. Fix a card labelled 'Nothing wrong' onto Jesus' cross. As Jesus promises one criminal that he will be in Paradise, swap the sign on Jesus' cross with that criminal's cross. The criminal was now the one who had done no wrong.

enough to tell them the bare facts that Jesus died, as is the case in the Gospel accounts. Children who have been part of a church for a long time should hear it in as refreshing a way as possible, using sound effects, visual images, video clips (but make sure the story is told accurately and appropriately), drama, puppets, repetition, light and colour or objects in a story bag. For more details read *Top Tips on Sharing Bible Stories* (SU) –see the inside front cover for details.

## Use of concrete language

Much of the Christian faith is about abstract concepts: sin, faith, even love. But abstract concepts are a challenge for children until they reach teenage years.

Take the traditional (not biblical) idea of 'asking Jesus into your heart'. This is an invitation to children to make Jesus the centre of their lives but some have asked how he gets there, does he need to be injected? And if you have a heart transplant, do you have to ask him in again? It is far better to ask if they would like Jesus to be their friend or simply to follow him like a supporter follows a football team or even to join Jesus' team. Note that the idea of being born again (John 3) to explain how to become a Christian is hard to grasp and only occurs in John 3, yet it has become a Christian cliché! Even Nicodemus could barely understand it!

In making abstract concepts tangible, we must not simplify them too much. For example, we often explain sin as doing naughty things but sin also includes spoiling relationships or ignoring God. It is anything that fails to meet God's standard, missing the mark.

**In reality...**
Be careful how you talk to children about responding to Jesus and his death on the cross. I often use the term 'friend of Jesus' when using the reconciliation model. I use the term 'follower' when using the Jesus Victor model. The word 'Christian' is often misunderstood, especially in a culture where ethnic identity is tied up with religious identity.

## Different contexts

No single explanation about Jesus' death on the cross will be right in every situation. The context in which you are talking must influence what you say.

### Church on Sunday
Most children in church on a Sunday will have some basic understanding of the fact that Jesus died on a cross. But a child from a Christian family may know facts of what happened *physically* and yet have no idea of the *spiritual* impact of Jesus' death or may never have thought about the implications for themselves. Children should be hearing about the cross in both all-age worship and in any regular Sunday children's group that they attend.

In all-age worship:

- Communication tends to be one-way, from leader to congregation, so all words need to be chosen with great care to communicate across the age groups.
- Keep to one main concept.
- Use simple, jargon-free language that can be understood by anyone. (Many adults benefit from hearing explanations to children of profound truths.)
- Use illustrations where possible – images or stories to build links between children and the truths being taught, such as one child acting as a go-between for two friends who have fallen out.
- Build links to and from other parts of the service – words of songs, Bible readings, particular elements of the service such as a confession which focuses upon sin and the need to ask for and receive forgiveness.
- Make the most of the opportunities presented by baptism and communion. Both these sacraments are packed with meaning and reflections of the cross (cleansing, death and resurrection, new covenant, body and blood). Link these both ways: use their meaning to build on the children's  understanding of the cross, and explain the sacraments in the light of what Jesus achieved on the cross.

In a children's group:
- Allow children to ask questions and discuss issues.
- Ask questions to assess the children's understanding. Whilst questions that have clear right and wrong answers are helpful for getting across facts, also ask open-ended, 'I wonder…' type questions.
- Without getting too complicated, set the explanation of the cross in the context of the whole Bible's message and, where appropriate, in relation to passages that have been covered recently in the curriculum.
- If possible, make use of more than one learning style to cater for all children – eg storytelling (aural), with pictures (visual), craft or drama (kinaesthetic). For more ideas, read *Top Tips on Communicating God in non-book ways* (SU).
- Include teaching about the cross at times of the year other than Easter. (This is also true of the Christmas story.) The message of the cross is central to the gospel, but children quickly tire of it if you bring it in every week.
- Be prepared to help children respond to the story in an appropriate way. That may not yet be what might be called a 'commitment'.

**Church, but not on Sunday**
Those with no previous church experience, who perhaps attend a midweek or holiday club, may have no knowledge at all of even the basic facts of Jesus' death on the cross. In addition to the above suggestions, consider the following:

In a regular midweek club:
- Help children understand the cross in relation to the rest of the Bible.
- Help them to understand what the cross means in practice. This is not just in formal 'presentations' but can be part of the way you deal with pastoral issues. The fact that Jesus is the victor can be very reassuring to a child who is being bullied; so too is the truth that God loved us so much that he acted to change things.
- Pick up on events or issues that arise in the club and link these – carefully, of course! – with teaching about the cross.
- These children may have no one at home who understands the meaning of the cross, so give them an opportunity to discuss and raise questions in the club. Facilitate this by having an 'ask-it basket', for children to put questions to be answered by leaders later in the session.

**Think about…**

How might a child experiencing a bereavement be helped by hearing about the cross…or a child who is at a time of transition or one who suffers from poor self-esteem?

Holiday clubs

Often at a holiday club there is a mix of children who attend church regularly, some with no church background but whom you know well, and others unused to church who are not known to you. It can be difficult to pitch things at the right level, so go for simplicity in general teaching and greater depth, where appropriate, in small groups. Avoid asking questions that put unchurched children at a disadvantage.

Churched children may feel the story is so familiar that they switch off or become disruptive because they are bored. Tell the Bible story with imagination, sharing your own enthusiasm and allowing them to get involved. Remember, a 10-year-old at a holiday club will not have heard about the cross as a 10-year-old. Last year they were nine! So this is new for them!

## School

You may have an opportunity in school to talk formally about the meaning of the cross in various settings:

- In a Christian club
- As part of an RE lesson
- In collective worship
- Linked to special occasions

You will need to keep to the boundaries set by legislation in terms of what can be said about Jesus' death on the cross. Physical details can be explained with the preface, 'The Bible says...' whilst it is probably better to introduce spiritual truths with the words, 'Christians believe...' It is vital to comply with this where children are present compulsorily. There is a little more leeway when children attend a voluntary Christian group, but many will be at the 'finding out about Jesus' stage. So do not make assumptions about their beliefs or agreement with Christian truths, and never put pressure on them.

In collective worship or RE lessons it is highly likely that children will be present from other faith backgrounds. In the classroom context it would make sense to teach the cross and its meaning as a Christian belief, recognising that others might not agree. You could look at the experience of Barabbas, a guilty person set free by the unconditional sacrificial death of Jesus. Be aware that Islam recognises Jesus as a prophet but not as the Son of God, so Muslim children would struggle to accept that his death has any impact on anyone's relationship with

God. (Most Muslims would believe that Jesus did not actually die.) Since Judaism does not recognise Jesus as the Messiah, Jewish children may not be as shocked at Jesus being killed. The charge against him of blasphemy would be acceptable to them.

Remember that it is *God's* work to bring a child to an awareness of who Jesus is; your role is to explain it simply and leave the rest to the Holy Spirit.

You may be asked to support a school through a crisis, such as the death of a pupil or member of staff. This calls for great sensitivity, but it may be appropriate to talk about the cross at such a time: Jesus understood the sadness of being separated from someone precious; he promised that he would take those who were his friends to be with him for ever. Choose your words with care: if, say, an adult who has openly denied God then dies, do not confuse matters by claiming promises for them that are clearly for those who have followed Jesus. Times like this require skill and integrity, and are all the more emotive when it is a child who has died. For more details of resources see page 32.

## Recognising children are children

A key factor in helping children to understand the death of Jesus is the strength and nature of your relationship with them. Trust and openness will allow them to ask questions or raise doubts.

Listen carefully to what they say. Try to work out what lies behind their questions and see things from their perspective. Avoid making assumptions about what they already know and understand; treat their questions seriously.

Explain in words and ideas that are appropriate for their age and background what Jesus' death means to you.

Often children will ask very specific questions which, if they are to be answered properly, require complex answers. For example, 'Why did Jesus die?' really needs an answer that begins with God and continues with Adam and Eve. But most children are not able to cope with more than a simple factual answer such as, 'The religious leaders of the day had him killed.' Talk only as much as the child can cope with, and then stop. Watch their face for signs that they have lost interest or have become confused.

If your conversation is part of ongoing work, talk more at another time. Even if this is a one-off conversation, remember that God is at work in the child and other people can fill in the gaps. Having said that, listen out for the Holy Spirit's prompting so that you do not stop short and miss the moment when a child is ready to hear more and make big decisions!

Pick up on those things that are relevant to the children in your group and use them to lead into teaching about the cross. Issues of justice or bullying make sense to children, as do punishment for breaking rules, the importance of defeating wrong and the need to restore broken friendships.

It is vital, wherever possible, to work with children's parents. Help them to talk with their children too.

**In reality…**
One church ran two evenings for parents, to support them as they nurtured the faith of their children. This included helping them to explain the meaning of the cross. For many parents this was valuable for their own faith!

# Culture

Just as pictures help children enjoy and remember a story, illustrations from life and links from culture help them understand the cross. Look for echoes in the news, events in their lives, or in familiar books or films that will help it make sense. They need to be the *right* books and events however, that are relevant to these children. For example, at the end of the 1980s the fall of the Berlin wall was a helpful illustration of freedom and reconciliation, but means nothing to today's children. However, despite them being written in the 1950s, many children still enjoy the *Narnia* books that are rich with imagery linked to Jesus' death.

If you are using news stories, consider these things:

- Is the event suitable to use with children of this age?
- Do the children understand enough of what is happening?
- Does the event adequately help to explain the cross? Will introducing it detract from the explanation or confuse the children?

If you are using the children's own experiences, consider if all the children have had that experience or can at least imagine what is involved in it; is it appropriate for the whole group? Will using it help explain the cross or change the focus away from it?

Stories work better if they are already well known to the majority of your group, as the children are then more likely to remember the link to the cross rather than just the story itself. Even if it is well known, tell it again. This will help any who have not heard it before, but also means that children hear the detail correctly and what you are referring to, in particular. If it is a long book, summarise the story and just read a relevant short section that sums up what you want to illustrate. Films can also be useful but tend to have a much shorter lifespan than books, so choose with care.

Below are some stories that echo the different explanations of Jesus' death. What others can you think of that reflect these truths?

- Jesus the Sacrifice: references in the *Harry Potter* books (JK Rowling) to Harry's mother dying in order to save him.
- Jesus the Rescuer: in the story of *Dogger* (Shirley Hughes), Dave's older sister gives up her newly-won teddy in order to get back Dogger, Dave's much-loved toy.
- Jesus the Reconciler: bringing people back to God – this will be familiar to most children from their playground and home experiences.
- Jesus the Victor: defeating the power of evil – in *The Lion, The Witch and The Wardrobe* (CS Lewis) Aslan is victorious over the White Witch and her powers.

Some of the books listed above are one of a series. Some children may have begun the series but not finished the entire set. So to increase the likelihood of more children knowing the piece to which you are referring - and to avoid giving away the end of the story for children who have not yet read that far! - take illustrations from the earlier books and take care not to spoil the story.

Children need to understand the cross in the context of God's love. Books such as *Guess How Much I Love You* (Sam

**Think about...**
If there is no suitable story, or the children are not keen readers, can you create one that fits the situation?

McBratney) and *No Matter What* (Debi Gliori) both express a depth of love in the parent-child relationship that echoes God's love.

## Helping children respond to the message of the cross

Some children will have lots of questions; others will want to become friends with Jesus and just need to know how to do this, while others will be attracted by the idea of joining a club! Listen to each child before launching into telling them what to do. It may be that you have explained the message to children all-together and offered to share more with them if they ask you. In which case, ask what they want to know, what they already understand and why they have come to talk with you.

Offering to help them pray a simple prayer of commitment or giving a booklet (such as *Me and Jesus* – see the inside back cover) may be helpful. The prayer of response suggestions after each of the four models on page 18 are simply a guide. We would not want to put words into a child's mouth that they do not understand or want to say.

It's best to talk one to one with each child, though this is not always possible. It's important not to go anywhere private or out of sight to talk. Find a quiet area where other people are, and sit in a way that is comfortable for the child. Don't pressurise the child for 'a decision'. You are helping them respond to God. If the Holy Spirit is at work, we can leave it up to him.

# TEN TOP TIPS

- Make sure you understand the cross yourself!

- Know the children you are talking to and be appropriate in the context where you are meeting them.

- Use concrete terms and keep it simple.

- Don't mix up ways of explaining the cross. If the Bible story is using one model for understanding the cross, stick with that. Even if it isn't, stick to one!

- Explain what children might do to respond to Jesus dying for them.

- Include the resurrection when you talk about the cross with children.

- Tell the story clearly and imaginatively, making sure you are not telling anything that a child might have to unlearn later.

- Children respond to the cross in a variety of ways and recognising their need for forgiveness may not be their response every time.

- Some children make a series of responses to Jesus over the course of their childhood. These may, or may not, grow into a commitment.

- It is God's Spirit who gives understanding and is at work in the life of a child or young person. You can't say everything about the cross in five minutes. Be aware that later in life children need to relate to all the models of understanding the cross.

# RESOURCES

### To use with children

SU Booklets for those who are interested in following Jesus:
*Friends with Jesus*, (for 5-7s); *Me and Jesus* (for 8-9s); *Jesus=Friendship forever* (for 10-12s)

Robert Willoughby, *So who is God?*, SU, 2006, 30 questions children ask about God, including those about the cross.

Steve Hutchinson, *So, why God?*, SU, 2007, 12 sessions for a discipleship programme.

Dave Godfrey, *Seaside Rock*, SU, 2003, holiday club programme on the life of Peter that explains the cross clearly.

Jean Elliott, *Clues2Use*, SU, 2005, 8 sessions for a midweek club which is focused around the *Jesus Quest DVD*.

Doug Swanney, *Xpedition Force*, SU, 2003, holiday club programme which follows the days leading up to the cross from Matthew's gospel.

### DVDs and video

*Mark Time*, SU, episode 5 *The Crucifixion*, 1989

*Jesus Quest*, Agape and SU with *Clues2Use* (see above), 2005, episode 7 *The Saviour*

*Wastewatchers* DVD, SU, 2007, episodes 4 and 5

*Xpedition Force* DVD, SU, 2006, all five episodes

### For adult leaders

I. Howard Marshall, *Aspects of the atonement: cross and resurrection in the reconciling of God and humanity*, Paternoster, 2007

John Stott, *The cross of Christ*, IVP, 2006

Tom Wright, *The cross and the colliery*, SPCK Publishing, 2007

Derek Tidball, *The message of the cross*, IVP, 2001

Janet Goodall, *Children and grieving*, SU, 1995

Christine Chapman, *Saying goodbye to Greg*, BRF, 2004